Softball Strength & Conditioning Log

This Book Belongs To:

_____

Visit http://elegantnotebooks.com for more
sports training books.

Training Log and Diary
Nutrition Log and Diary
Strength and Conditioning Log and Diary

| DATE: | | WEEK: | | WEIGHT: | |

Warm Up/ Stretching   Duration:

Exercise		Set 1	Set 2	Set 3	Set 4	Set 5
	Weight					
	Reps					
	Weight					
	Reps					
	Weight					
	Reps					
	Weight					
	Reps					
	Weight					
	Reps					
	Weight					
	Reps					
	Weight					
	Reps					
	Weight					
	Reps					
	Weight					
	Reps					
	Weight					
	Reps					
	Weight					
	Reps					
	Weight					
	Reps					

CARDIO WORKOUT

Exercise	Duration	Pace	Heart Rate	Calories

WATER   1 cup per circle
(1 cup = 8 ounces ~ 240ml)   ○ ○ ○ ○ ○ ○ ○ ○ ○ ○ ○ ○ ○ ○ ○ ○ ○

DATE: | **WEEK:** | **WEIGHT:**

Warm Up/ Stretching **Duration:**

Exercise		Set 1	Set 2	Set 3	Set 4	Set 5
	Weight					
	Reps					
	Weight					
	Reps					
	Weight					
	Reps					
	Weight					
	Reps					
	Weight					
	Reps					
	Weight					
	Reps					
	Weight					
	Reps					
	Weight					
	Reps					
	Weight					
	Reps					
	Weight					
	Reps					
	Weight					
	Reps					
	Weight					
	Reps					

CARDIO WORKOUT

Exercise	Duration	Pace	Heart Rate	Calories

WATER   1 cup per circle
(1 cup = 8 ounces ~ 240ml)   ○ ○ ○ ○ ○ ○ ○ ○ ○ ○ ○ ○ ○ ○ ○

DATE:	WEEK:	WEIGHT:

Warm Up/ Stretching	Duration:

Exercise		Set 1	Set 2	Set 3	Set 4	Set 5
	Weight					
	Reps					
	Weight					
	Reps					
	Weight					
	Reps					
	Weight					
	Reps					
	Weight					
	Reps					
	Weight					
	Reps					
	Weight					
	Reps					
	Weight					
	Reps					
	Weight					
	Reps					
	Weight					
	Reps					
	Weight					
	Reps					
	Weight					
	Reps					

CARDIO WORKOUT

Exercise	Duration	Pace	Heart Rate	Calories

WATER   1 cup per circle
(1 cup = 8 ounces ~ 240ml)   ○○○○○○○○○○○○○○○○○○

DATE:	WEEK:	WEIGHT:

Warm Up/ Stretching   Duration:

Exercise		Set 1	Set 2	Set 3	Set 4	Set 5
	Weight					
	Reps					
	Weight					
	Reps					
	Weight					
	Reps					
	Weight					
	Reps					
	Weight					
	Reps					
	Weight					
	Reps					
	Weight					
	Reps					
	Weight					
	Reps					
	Weight					
	Reps					
	Weight					
	Reps					
	Weight					
	Reps					
	Weight					
	Reps					

CARDIO WORKOUT

Exercise	Duration	Pace	Heart Rate	Calories

WATER   1 cup per circle
(1 cup = 8 ounces ~ 240ml)   ○ ○ ○ ○ ○ ○ ○ ○ ○ ○ ○ ○ ○ ○ ○ ○

DATE:		WEEK:		WEIGHT:	

Warm Up/ Stretching				Duration:	

Exercise		Set 1	Set 2	Set 3	Set 4	Set 5
	Weight					
	Reps					
	Weight					
	Reps					
	Weight					
	Reps					
	Weight					
	Reps					
	Weight					
	Reps					
	Weight					
	Reps					
	Weight					
	Reps					
	Weight					
	Reps					
	Weight					
	Reps					
	Weight					
	Reps					
	Weight					
	Reps					
	Weight					
	Reps					

CARDIO WORKOUT

Exercise	Duration	Pace	Heart Rate	Calories

WATER   1 cup per circle
(1 cup = 8 ounces ~ 240ml)   ○ ○ ○ ○ ○ ○ ○ ○ ○ ○ ○ ○ ○ ○ ○ ○

DATE: [ ] **WEEK:** [ ] **WEIGHT:** [ ]

Warm Up/ Stretching   Duration: [ ]

Exercise		Set 1	Set 2	Set 3	Set 4	Set 5
	Weight					
	Reps					
	Weight					
	Reps					
	Weight					
	Reps					
	Weight					
	Reps					
	Weight					
	Reps					
	Weight					
	Reps					
	Weight					
	Reps					
	Weight					
	Reps					
	Weight					
	Reps					
	Weight					
	Reps					
	Weight					
	Reps					
	Weight					
	Reps					

CARDIO WORKOUT

Exercise	Duration	Pace	Heart Rate	Calories

WATER   1 cup per circle
(1 cup = 8 ounces ~ 240ml)   ○ ○ ○ ○ ○ ○ ○ ○ ○ ○ ○ ○ ○ ○ ○ ○ ○ ○ ○

DATE:	WEEK:	WEIGHT:

Warm Up/ Stretching   Duration:

Exercise		Set 1	Set 2	Set 3	Set 4	Set 5
	Weight					
	Reps					
	Weight					
	Reps					
	Weight					
	Reps					
	Weight					
	Reps					
	Weight					
	Reps					
	Weight					
	Reps					
	Weight					
	Reps					
	Weight					
	Reps					
	Weight					
	Reps					
	Weight					
	Reps					
	Weight					
	Reps					
	Weight					
	Reps					

CARDIO WORKOUT

Exercise	Duration	Pace	Heart Rate	Calories

WATER   1 cup per circle
(1 cup = 8 ounces ~ 240ml)   ○○○○○○○○○○○○○○○○○

DATE:		WEEK:		WEIGHT:	

Warm Up/ Stretching Duration: _____

Exercise		Set 1	Set 2	Set 3	Set 4	Set 5
	Weight					
	Reps					
	Weight					
	Reps					
	Weight					
	Reps					
	Weight					
	Reps					
	Weight					
	Reps					
	Weight					
	Reps					
	Weight					
	Reps					
	Weight					
	Reps					
	Weight					
	Reps					
	Weight					
	Reps					
	Weight					
	Reps					
	Weight					
	Reps					

CARDIO WORKOUT

Exercise	Duration	Pace	Heart Rate	Calories

WATER   1 cup per circle
(1 cup = 8 ounces ~ 240ml)   ○ ○ ○ ○ ○ ○ ○ ○ ○ ○ ○ ○ ○ ○ ○ ○

DATE:	WEEK:	WEIGHT:

Warm Up/ Stretching	Duration:

Exercise		Set 1	Set 2	Set 3	Set 4	Set 5
	Weight					
	Reps					
	Weight					
	Reps					
	Weight					
	Reps					
	Weight					
	Reps					
	Weight					
	Reps					
	Weight					
	Reps					
	Weight					
	Reps					
	Weight					
	Reps					
	Weight					
	Reps					
	Weight					
	Reps					
	Weight					
	Reps					
	Weight					
	Reps					

CARDIO WORKOUT

Exercise	Duration	Pace	Heart Rate	Calories

WATER   1 cup per circle
(1 cup = 8 ounces ~ 240ml)   ○○○○○○○○○○○○○○○○○

DATE:	WEEK:	WEIGHT:

Warm Up/ Stretching   **Duration:**

Exercise		Set 1	Set 2	Set 3	Set 4	Set 5
	Weight					
	Reps					
	Weight					
	Reps					
	Weight					
	Reps					
	Weight					
	Reps					
	Weight					
	Reps					
	Weight					
	Reps					
	Weight					
	Reps					
	Weight					
	Reps					
	Weight					
	Reps					
	Weight					
	Reps					
	Weight					
	Reps					
	Weight					
	Reps					

CARDIO WORKOUT

Exercise	Duration	Pace	Heart Rate	Calories

WATER   1 cup per circle
(1 cup = 8 ounces ~ 240ml)   ○ ○ ○ ○ ○ ○ ○ ○ ○ ○ ○ ○ ○ ○ ○

DATE:		WEEK:		WEIGHT:	

Warm Up/ Stretching	Duration:

Exercise		Set 1	Set 2	Set 3	Set 4	Set 5
	Weight					
	Reps					
	Weight					
	Reps					
	Weight					
	Reps					
	Weight					
	Reps					
	Weight					
	Reps					
	Weight					
	Reps					
	Weight					
	Reps					
	Weight					
	Reps					
	Weight					
	Reps					
	Weight					
	Reps					
	Weight					
	Reps					
	Weight					
	Reps					

CARDIO WORKOUT

Exercise	Duration	Pace	Heart Rate	Calories

WATER   1 cup per circle
(1 cup = 8 ounces ~ 240ml)   ○○○○○○○○○○○○○○○○○○

DATE:		WEEK:		WEIGHT:	

Warm Up/ Stretching   **Duration:**

Exercise		Set 1	Set 2	Set 3	Set 4	Set 5
	Weight					
	Reps					
	Weight					
	Reps					
	Weight					
	Reps					
	Weight					
	Reps					
	Weight					
	Reps					
	Weight					
	Reps					
	Weight					
	Reps					
	Weight					
	Reps					
	Weight					
	Reps					
	Weight					
	Reps					
	Weight					
	Reps					
	Weight					
	Reps					

CARDIO WORKOUT

Exercise	Duration	Pace	Heart Rate	Calories

WATER   1 cup per circle
(1 cup = 8 ounces ~ 240ml)   ○ ○ ○ ○ ○ ○ ○ ○ ○ ○ ○ ○ ○ ○ ○ ○ ○

DATE:	WEEK:	WEIGHT:

Warm Up/ Stretching	Duration:

Exercise		Set 1	Set 2	Set 3	Set 4	Set 5
	Weight					
	Reps					
	Weight					
	Reps					
	Weight					
	Reps					
	Weight					
	Reps					
	Weight					
	Reps					
	Weight					
	Reps					
	Weight					
	Reps					
	Weight					
	Reps					
	Weight					
	Reps					
	Weight					
	Reps					
	Weight					
	Reps					
	Weight					
	Reps					

CARDIO WORKOUT

Exercise	Duration	Pace	Heart Rate	Calories

WATER   1 cup per circle
(1 cup = 8 ounces ~ 240ml)   ○○○○○○○○○○○○○○○○

DATE:	WEEK:	WEIGHT:

Warm Up/ Stretching　　　　　　　　　　　**Duration:**

Exercise		Set 1	Set 2	Set 3	Set 4	Set 5
	Weight					
	Reps					
	Weight					
	Reps					
	Weight					
	Reps					
	Weight					
	Reps					
	Weight					
	Reps					
	Weight					
	Reps					
	Weight					
	Reps					
	Weight					
	Reps					
	Weight					
	Reps					
	Weight					
	Reps					
	Weight					
	Reps					
	Weight					
	Reps					

CARDIO WORKOUT

Exercise	Duration	Pace	Heart Rate	Calories

WATER　　1 cup per circle
(1 cup = 8 ounces ~ 240ml)　　○○○○○○○○○○○○○○○○○○

DATE: [   ]   **WEEK:** [   ]   **WEIGHT:** [   ]

Warm Up/ Stretching					**Duration:** [ ]

Exercise		Set 1	Set 2	Set 3	Set 4	Set 5
	Weight					
	Reps					
	Weight					
	Reps					
	Weight					
	Reps					
	Weight					
	Reps					
	Weight					
	Reps					
	Weight					
	Reps					
	Weight					
	Reps					
	Weight					
	Reps					
	Weight					
	Reps					
	Weight					
	Reps					
	Weight					
	Reps					
	Weight					
	Reps					

CARDIO WORKOUT

Exercise	Duration	Pace	Heart Rate	Calories

WATER   1 cup per circle
(1 cup = 8 ounces ~ 240ml)   ○○○○○○○○○○○○○○○○○○

DATE:		WEEK:		WEIGHT:	

Warm Up/ Stretching Duration: _____

Exercise		Set 1	Set 2	Set 3	Set 4	Set 5
	Weight					
	Reps					
	Weight					
	Reps					
	Weight					
	Reps					
	Weight					
	Reps					
	Weight					
	Reps					
	Weight					
	Reps					
	Weight					
	Reps					
	Weight					
	Reps					
	Weight					
	Reps					
	Weight					
	Reps					
	Weight					
	Reps					
	Weight					
	Reps					

CARDIO WORKOUT

Exercise	Duration	Pace	Heart Rate	Calories

WATER   1 cup per circle
(1 cup = 8 ounces ~ 240ml)   ○○○○○○○○○○○○○○○○○○

DATE:	WEEK:	WEIGHT:

Warm Up/ Stretching	Duration:

Exercise		Set 1	Set 2	Set 3	Set 4	Set 5
	Weight					
	Reps					
	Weight					
	Reps					
	Weight					
	Reps					
	Weight					
	Reps					
	Weight					
	Reps					
	Weight					
	Reps					
	Weight					
	Reps					
	Weight					
	Reps					
	Weight					
	Reps					
	Weight					
	Reps					
	Weight					
	Reps					
	Weight					
	Reps					
	Weight					
	Reps					

CARDIO WORKOUT

Exercise	Duration	Pace	Heart Rate	Calories

WATER   1 cup per circle
(1 cup = 8 ounces ~ 240ml)   ○○○○○○○○○○○○○○○○

DATE:		WEEK:		WEIGHT:	

Warm Up/ Stretching   Duration: [ ]

Exercise		Set 1	Set 2	Set 3	Set 4	Set 5
	Weight					
	Reps					
	Weight					
	Reps					
	Weight					
	Reps					
	Weight					
	Reps					
	Weight					
	Reps					
	Weight					
	Reps					
	Weight					
	Reps					
	Weight					
	Reps					
	Weight					
	Reps					
	Weight					
	Reps					
	Weight					
	Reps					
	Weight					
	Reps					

CARDIO WORKOUT

Exercise	Duration	Pace	Heart Rate	Calories

WATER   1 cup per circle
(1 cup = 8 ounces ~ 240ml)   ○○○○○○○○○○○○○○○○○○

| DATE: | WEEK: | WEIGHT: |

Warm Up/ Stretching Duration:

Exercise		Set 1	Set 2	Set 3	Set 4	Set 5
	Weight					
	Reps					
	Weight					
	Reps					
	Weight					
	Reps					
	Weight					
	Reps					
	Weight					
	Reps					
	Weight					
	Reps					
	Weight					
	Reps					
	Weight					
	Reps					
	Weight					
	Reps					
	Weight					
	Reps					
	Weight					
	Reps					
	Weight					
	Reps					

CARDIO WORKOUT

Exercise	Duration	Pace	Heart Rate	Calories

WATER   1 cup per circle
(1 cup = 8 ounces ~ 240ml)   ○○○○○○○○○○○○○○○○○

DATE:	WEEK:	WEIGHT:

Warm Up/ Stretching Duration:

Exercise		Set 1	Set 2	Set 3	Set 4	Set 5
	Weight					
	Reps					
	Weight					
	Reps					
	Weight					
	Reps					
	Weight					
	Reps					
	Weight					
	Reps					
	Weight					
	Reps					
	Weight					
	Reps					
	Weight					
	Reps					
	Weight					
	Reps					
	Weight					
	Reps					
	Weight					
	Reps					
	Weight					
	Reps					

CARDIO WORKOUT

Exercise	Duration	Pace	Heart Rate	Calories

WATER   1 cup per circle
(1 cup = 8 ounces ~ 240ml)   ○ ○ ○ ○ ○ ○ ○ ○ ○ ○ ○ ○ ○ ○ ○ ○

DATE:	WEEK:	WEIGHT:

Warm Up/ Stretching Duration:

Exercise		Set 1	Set 2	Set 3	Set 4	Set 5
	Weight					
	Reps					
	Weight					
	Reps					
	Weight					
	Reps					
	Weight					
	Reps					
	Weight					
	Reps					
	Weight					
	Reps					
	Weight					
	Reps					
	Weight					
	Reps					
	Weight					
	Reps					
	Weight					
	Reps					
	Weight					
	Reps					
	Weight					
	Reps					

CARDIO WORKOUT

Exercise	Duration	Pace	Heart Rate	Calories

WATER 1 cup per circle
(1 cup = 8 ounces ~ 240ml) ○○○○○○○○○○○○○○○○

DATE:	WEEK:	WEIGHT:

Warm Up/ Stretching Duration:

Exercise		Set 1	Set 2	Set 3	Set 4	Set 5
	Weight					
	Reps					
	Weight					
	Reps					
	Weight					
	Reps					
	Weight					
	Reps					
	Weight					
	Reps					
	Weight					
	Reps					
	Weight					
	Reps					
	Weight					
	Reps					
	Weight					
	Reps					
	Weight					
	Reps					
	Weight					
	Reps					
	Weight					
	Reps					

CARDIO WORKOUT

Exercise	Duration	Pace	Heart Rate	Calories

WATER   1 cup per circle
(1 cup = 8 ounces ~ 240ml)   ○ ○ ○ ○ ○ ○ ○ ○ ○ ○ ○ ○ ○ ○ ○ ○ ○ ○

DATE:		WEEK:		WEIGHT:	

Warm Up/ Stretching		Duration:	

Exercise		Set 1	Set 2	Set 3	Set 4	Set 5
	Weight					
	Reps					
	Weight					
	Reps					
	Weight					
	Reps					
	Weight					
	Reps					
	Weight					
	Reps					
	Weight					
	Reps					
	Weight					
	Reps					
	Weight					
	Reps					
	Weight					
	Reps					
	Weight					
	Reps					
	Weight					
	Reps					
	Weight					
	Reps					

CARDIO WORKOUT

Exercise	Duration	Pace	Heart Rate	Calories

WATER   1 cup per circle
(1 cup = 8 ounces ~ 240ml)

○ ○ ○ ○ ○ ○ ○ ○ ○ ○ ○ ○ ○ ○ ○

DATE: | **WEEK:** | **WEIGHT:**

Warm Up/ Stretching **Duration:**

Exercise		Set 1	Set 2	Set 3	Set 4	Set 5
	Weight					
	Reps					
	Weight					
	Reps					
	Weight					
	Reps					
	Weight					
	Reps					
	Weight					
	Reps					
	Weight					
	Reps					
	Weight					
	Reps					
	Weight					
	Reps					
	Weight					
	Reps					
	Weight					
	Reps					
	Weight					
	Reps					
	Weight					
	Reps					

CARDIO WORKOUT

Exercise	Duration	Pace	Heart Rate	Calories

WATER   1 cup per circle
(1 cup = 8 ounces ~ 240ml)   ○ ○ ○ ○ ○ ○ ○ ○ ○ ○ ○ ○ ○ ○ ○ ○

DATE: _____   **WEEK:** _____   **WEIGHT:** _____

| Warm Up/ Stretching | | | | **Duration:** | | |

Exercise		Set 1	Set 2	Set 3	Set 4	Set 5
	Weight					
	Reps					
	Weight					
	Reps					
	Weight					
	Reps					
	Weight					
	Reps					
	Weight					
	Reps					
	Weight					
	Reps					
	Weight					
	Reps					
	Weight					
	Reps					
	Weight					
	Reps					
	Weight					
	Reps					
	Weight					
	Reps					
	Weight					
	Reps					

CARDIO WORKOUT

Exercise	Duration	Pace	Heart Rate	Calories

WATER   1 cup per circle
(1 cup = 8 ounces ~ 240ml)   ◯◯◯◯◯◯◯◯◯◯◯◯◯◯◯◯

DATE:	WEEK:	WEIGHT:

Warm Up/ Stretching   Duration:

Exercise		Set 1	Set 2	Set 3	Set 4	Set 5
	Weight					
	Reps					
	Weight					
	Reps					
	Weight					
	Reps					
	Weight					
	Reps					
	Weight					
	Reps					
	Weight					
	Reps					
	Weight					
	Reps					
	Weight					
	Reps					
	Weight					
	Reps					
	Weight					
	Reps					
	Weight					
	Reps					
	Weight					
	Reps					

CARDIO WORKOUT

Exercise	Duration	Pace	Heart Rate	Calories

WATER   1 cup per circle
(1 cup = 8 ounces ~ 240ml)   ○○○○○○○○○○○○○○○○○

DATE:		WEEK:		WEIGHT:	

Warm Up/ Stretching   Duration: [ ]

Exercise		Set 1	Set 2	Set 3	Set 4	Set 5
	Weight					
	Reps					
	Weight					
	Reps					
	Weight					
	Reps					
	Weight					
	Reps					
	Weight					
	Reps					
	Weight					
	Reps					
	Weight					
	Reps					
	Weight					
	Reps					
	Weight					
	Reps					
	Weight					
	Reps					
	Weight					
	Reps					
	Weight					
	Reps					

CARDIO WORKOUT

Exercise	Duration	Pace	Heart Rate	Calories

WATER   1 cup per circle
(1 cup = 8 ounces ~ 240ml)   ○ ○ ○ ○ ○ ○ ○ ○ ○ ○ ○ ○ ○ ○ ○ ○

DATE: [ ] **WEEK:** [ ] **WEIGHT:** [ ]

Warm Up/ Stretching   **Duration:** [ ]

Exercise		Set 1	Set 2	Set 3	Set 4	Set 5
	Weight					
	Reps					
	Weight					
	Reps					
	Weight					
	Reps					
	Weight					
	Reps					
	Weight					
	Reps					
	Weight					
	Reps					
	Weight					
	Reps					
	Weight					
	Reps					
	Weight					
	Reps					
	Weight					
	Reps					
	Weight					
	Reps					
	Weight					
	Reps					

CARDIO WORKOUT

Exercise	Duration	Pace	Heart Rate	Calories

WATER   1 cup per circle
(1 cup = 8 ounces ~ 240ml)   ○ ○ ○ ○ ○ ○ ○ ○ ○ ○ ○ ○ ○ ○ ○ ○

DATE:		WEEK:		WEIGHT:	

Warm Up/ Stretching Duration:

Exercise		Set 1	Set 2	Set 3	Set 4	Set 5
	Weight					
	Reps					
	Weight					
	Reps					
	Weight					
	Reps					
	Weight					
	Reps					
	Weight					
	Reps					
	Weight					
	Reps					
	Weight					
	Reps					
	Weight					
	Reps					
	Weight					
	Reps					
	Weight					
	Reps					
	Weight					
	Reps					
	Weight					
	Reps					

CARDIO WORKOUT

Exercise	Duration	Pace	Heart Rate	Calories

WATER   1 cup per circle
(1 cup = 8 ounces ~ 240ml)   ○ ○ ○ ○ ○ ○ ○ ○ ○ ○ ○ ○ ○ ○ ○ ○

DATE:		WEEK:		WEIGHT:	

Warm Up/ Stretching Duration: [ ]

Exercise		Set 1	Set 2	Set 3	Set 4	Set 5
	Weight					
	Reps					
	Weight					
	Reps					
	Weight					
	Reps					
	Weight					
	Reps					
	Weight					
	Reps					
	Weight					
	Reps					
	Weight					
	Reps					
	Weight					
	Reps					
	Weight					
	Reps					
	Weight					
	Reps					
	Weight					
	Reps					
	Weight					
	Reps					

CARDIO WORKOUT

Exercise	Duration	Pace	Heart Rate	Calories

WATER 1 cup per circle
(1 cup = 8 ounces ~ 240ml)   ○○○○○○○○○○○○○○○○○○

DATE:		WEEK:		WEIGHT:	

Warm Up/ Stretching	Duration:

Exercise		Set 1	Set 2	Set 3	Set 4	Set 5
	Weight					
	Reps					
	Weight					
	Reps					
	Weight					
	Reps					
	Weight					
	Reps					
	Weight					
	Reps					
	Weight					
	Reps					
	Weight					
	Reps					
	Weight					
	Reps					
	Weight					
	Reps					
	Weight					
	Reps					
	Weight					
	Reps					
	Weight					
	Reps					

CARDIO WORKOUT

Exercise	Duration	Pace	Heart Rate	Calories

WATER   1 cup per circle
(1 cup = 8 ounces ~ 240ml)   ○○○○○○○○○○○○○○○○

DATE:		WEEK:		WEIGHT:	

Warm Up/ Stretching   **Duration:** [ ]

Exercise		Set 1	Set 2	Set 3	Set 4	Set 5
	Weight					
	Reps					
	Weight					
	Reps					
	Weight					
	Reps					
	Weight					
	Reps					
	Weight					
	Reps					
	Weight					
	Reps					
	Weight					
	Reps					
	Weight					
	Reps					
	Weight					
	Reps					
	Weight					
	Reps					
	Weight					
	Reps					
	Weight					
	Reps					

CARDIO WORKOUT

Exercise	Duration	Pace	Heart Rate	Calories

WATER   1 cup per circle
(1 cup = 8 ounces ~ 240ml)   ○○○○○○○○○○○○○○○○○○

DATE:		WEEK:		WEIGHT:	

Warm Up/ Stretching		Duration:	

Exercise		Set 1	Set 2	Set 3	Set 4	Set 5
	Weight					
	Reps					
	Weight					
	Reps					
	Weight					
	Reps					
	Weight					
	Reps					
	Weight					
	Reps					
	Weight					
	Reps					
	Weight					
	Reps					
	Weight					
	Reps					
	Weight					
	Reps					
	Weight					
	Reps					
	Weight					
	Reps					
	Weight					
	Reps					

CARDIO WORKOUT

Exercise	Duration	Pace	Heart Rate	Calories

WATER   1 cup per circle
(1 cup = 8 ounces ~ 240ml)   ○○○○○○○○○○○○○○○○○

DATE: [ ] **WEEK:** [ ] **WEIGHT:** [ ]

| Warm Up/ Stretching | | Duration: [ ] |

Exercise		Set 1	Set 2	Set 3	Set 4	Set 5
	Weight					
	Reps					
	Weight					
	Reps					
	Weight					
	Reps					
	Weight					
	Reps					
	Weight					
	Reps					
	Weight					
	Reps					
	Weight					
	Reps					
	Weight					
	Reps					
	Weight					
	Reps					
	Weight					
	Reps					
	Weight					
	Reps					
	Weight					
	Reps					

CARDIO WORKOUT

Exercise	Duration	Pace	Heart Rate	Calories

WATER   1 cup per circle
(1 cup = 8 ounces ~ 240ml)   ○ ○ ○ ○ ○ ○ ○ ○ ○ ○ ○ ○ ○ ○ ○ ○

DATE:	WEEK:	WEIGHT:

Warm Up/ Stretching   **Duration:**

Exercise		Set 1	Set 2	Set 3	Set 4	Set 5
	Weight					
	Reps					
	Weight					
	Reps					
	Weight					
	Reps					
	Weight					
	Reps					
	Weight					
	Reps					
	Weight					
	Reps					
	Weight					
	Reps					
	Weight					
	Reps					
	Weight					
	Reps					
	Weight					
	Reps					
	Weight					
	Reps					
	Weight					
	Reps					

CARDIO WORKOUT

Exercise	Duration	Pace	Heart Rate	Calories

WATER   1 cup per circle
(1 cup = 8 ounces ~ 240ml)   ○○○○○○○○○○○○○○○

DATE:	WEEK:	WEIGHT:

Warm Up/ Stretching   Duration:

Exercise		Set 1	Set 2	Set 3	Set 4	Set 5
	Weight					
	Reps					
	Weight					
	Reps					
	Weight					
	Reps					
	Weight					
	Reps					
	Weight					
	Reps					
	Weight					
	Reps					
	Weight					
	Reps					
	Weight					
	Reps					
	Weight					
	Reps					
	Weight					
	Reps					
	Weight					
	Reps					
	Weight					
	Reps					

CARDIO WORKOUT

Exercise	Duration	Pace	Heart Rate	Calories

WATER   1 cup per circle
(1 cup = 8 ounces ~ 240ml)   ○ ○ ○ ○ ○ ○ ○ ○ ○ ○ ○ ○ ○ ○ ○ ○ ○

DATE:		WEEK:		WEIGHT:	

Warm Up/ Stretching	Duration:	

Exercise		Set 1	Set 2	Set 3	Set 4	Set 5
	Weight					
	Reps					
	Weight					
	Reps					
	Weight					
	Reps					
	Weight					
	Reps					
	Weight					
	Reps					
	Weight					
	Reps					
	Weight					
	Reps					
	Weight					
	Reps					
	Weight					
	Reps					
	Weight					
	Reps					
	Weight					
	Reps					
	Weight					
	Reps					

CARDIO WORKOUT

Exercise	Duration	Pace	Heart Rate	Calories

WATER   1 cup per circle
(1 cup = 8 ounces ~ 240ml)   ○○○○○○○○○○○○○○○○○

DATE:	WEEK:	WEIGHT:

Warm Up/ Stretching   **Duration:**

Exercise		Set 1	Set 2	Set 3	Set 4	Set 5
	Weight					
	Reps					
	Weight					
	Reps					
	Weight					
	Reps					
	Weight					
	Reps					
	Weight					
	Reps					
	Weight					
	Reps					
	Weight					
	Reps					
	Weight					
	Reps					
	Weight					
	Reps					
	Weight					
	Reps					
	Weight					
	Reps					
	Weight					
	Reps					

CARDIO WORKOUT

Exercise	Duration	Pace	Heart Rate	Calories

WATER   1 cup per circle
(1 cup = 8 ounces ~ 240ml)   ○ ○ ○ ○ ○ ○ ○ ○ ○ ○ ○ ○ ○ ○ ○ ○

DATE:	WEEK:	WEIGHT:

Warm Up/ Stretching		Duration:

Exercise		Set 1	Set 2	Set 3	Set 4	Set 5
	Weight					
	Reps					
	Weight					
	Reps					
	Weight					
	Reps					
	Weight					
	Reps					
	Weight					
	Reps					
	Weight					
	Reps					
	Weight					
	Reps					
	Weight					
	Reps					
	Weight					
	Reps					
	Weight					
	Reps					
	Weight					
	Reps					
	Weight					
	Reps					

CARDIO WORKOUT

Exercise	Duration	Pace	Heart Rate	Calories

WATER   1 cup per circle
(1 cup = 8 ounces ~ 240ml)   ○ ○ ○ ○ ○ ○ ○ ○ ○ ○ ○ ○ ○ ○ ○ ○

DATE:		WEEK:		WEIGHT:	

Warm Up/ Stretching   **Duration:** [ ]

Exercise		Set 1	Set 2	Set 3	Set 4	Set 5
	Weight					
	Reps					
	Weight					
	Reps					
	Weight					
	Reps					
	Weight					
	Reps					
	Weight					
	Reps					
	Weight					
	Reps					
	Weight					
	Reps					
	Weight					
	Reps					
	Weight					
	Reps					
	Weight					
	Reps					
	Weight					
	Reps					
	Weight					
	Reps					

CARDIO WORKOUT

Exercise	Duration	Pace	Heart Rate	Calories

WATER   1 cup per circle
(1 cup = 8 ounces ~ 240ml)   ○○○○○○○○○○○○○○○○○

DATE:		WEEK:		WEIGHT:	

Warm Up/ Stretching	Duration:

Exercise		Set 1	Set 2	Set 3	Set 4	Set 5
	Weight					
	Reps					
	Weight					
	Reps					
	Weight					
	Reps					
	Weight					
	Reps					
	Weight					
	Reps					
	Weight					
	Reps					
	Weight					
	Reps					
	Weight					
	Reps					
	Weight					
	Reps					
	Weight					
	Reps					
	Weight					
	Reps					
	Weight					
	Reps					

CARDIO WORKOUT

Exercise	Duration	Pace	Heart Rate	Calories

WATER   1 cup per circle
(1 cup = 8 ounces ~ 240ml)   ○○○○○○○○○○○○○○○○○○

DATE:		WEEK:		WEIGHT:	

Warm Up/ Stretching   **Duration:** [   ]

Exercise		Set 1	Set 2	Set 3	Set 4	Set 5
	Weight					
	Reps					
	Weight					
	Reps					
	Weight					
	Reps					
	Weight					
	Reps					
	Weight					
	Reps					
	Weight					
	Reps					
	Weight					
	Reps					
	Weight					
	Reps					
	Weight					
	Reps					
	Weight					
	Reps					
	Weight					
	Reps					
	Weight					
	Reps					

CARDIO WORKOUT

Exercise	Duration	Pace	Heart Rate	Calories

WATER   1 cup per circle
(1 cup = 8 ounces ~ 240ml)   ○ ○ ○ ○ ○ ○ ○ ○ ○ ○ ○ ○ ○ ○ ○ ○

DATE: | **WEEK:** | **WEIGHT:**

| Warm Up/ Stretching | | | Duration: | |

Exercise		Set 1	Set 2	Set 3	Set 4	Set 5
	Weight					
	Reps					
	Weight					
	Reps					
	Weight					
	Reps					
	Weight					
	Reps					
	Weight					
	Reps					
	Weight					
	Reps					
	Weight					
	Reps					
	Weight					
	Reps					
	Weight					
	Reps					
	Weight					
	Reps					
	Weight					
	Reps					
	Weight					
	Reps					

CARDIO WORKOUT

Exercise	Duration	Pace	Heart Rate	Calories

WATER   1 cup per circle
(1 cup = 8 ounces ~ 240ml)   ○ ○ ○ ○ ○ ○ ○ ○ ○ ○ ○ ○ ○ ○ ○ ○ ○ ○

DATE:	WEEK:	WEIGHT:

Warm Up/ Stretching   Duration: [   ]

Exercise		Set 1	Set 2	Set 3	Set 4	Set 5
	Weight					
	Reps					
	Weight					
	Reps					
	Weight					
	Reps					
	Weight					
	Reps					
	Weight					
	Reps					
	Weight					
	Reps					
	Weight					
	Reps					
	Weight					
	Reps					
	Weight					
	Reps					
	Weight					
	Reps					
	Weight					
	Reps					
	Weight					
	Reps					

CARDIO WORKOUT

Exercise	Duration	Pace	Heart Rate	Calories

WATER   1 cup per circle
(1 cup = 8 ounces ~ 240ml)   ◯ ◯ ◯ ◯ ◯ ◯ ◯ ◯ ◯ ◯ ◯ ◯ ◯ ◯ ◯

DATE:		WEEK:		WEIGHT:	

Warm Up/ Stretching Duration: [ ]

Exercise		Set 1	Set 2	Set 3	Set 4	Set 5
	Weight					
	Reps					
	Weight					
	Reps					
	Weight					
	Reps					
	Weight					
	Reps					
	Weight					
	Reps					
	Weight					
	Reps					
	Weight					
	Reps					
	Weight					
	Reps					
	Weight					
	Reps					
	Weight					
	Reps					
	Weight					
	Reps					
	Weight					
	Reps					

CARDIO WORKOUT

Exercise	Duration	Pace	Heart Rate	Calories

WATER   1 cup per circle
(1 cup = 8 ounces ~ 240ml)   ○ ○ ○ ○ ○ ○ ○ ○ ○ ○ ○ ○ ○ ○ ○

DATE:	WEEK:	WEIGHT:

Warm Up/ Stretching   Duration:

Exercise		Set 1	Set 2	Set 3	Set 4	Set 5
	Weight					
	Reps					
	Weight					
	Reps					
	Weight					
	Reps					
	Weight					
	Reps					
	Weight					
	Reps					
	Weight					
	Reps					
	Weight					
	Reps					
	Weight					
	Reps					
	Weight					
	Reps					
	Weight					
	Reps					
	Weight					
	Reps					
	Weight					
	Reps					

CARDIO WORKOUT

Exercise	Duration	Pace	Heart Rate	Calories

WATER   1 cup per circle
(1 cup = 8 ounces ~ 240ml)   ○○○○○○○○○○○○○○○○○○

DATE:		WEEK:		WEIGHT:	

Warm Up/ Stretching	Duration:

Exercise		Set 1	Set 2	Set 3	Set 4	Set 5
	Weight					
	Reps					
	Weight					
	Reps					
	Weight					
	Reps					
	Weight					
	Reps					
	Weight					
	Reps					
	Weight					
	Reps					
	Weight					
	Reps					
	Weight					
	Reps					
	Weight					
	Reps					
	Weight					
	Reps					
	Weight					
	Reps					
	Weight					
	Reps					
	Weight					
	Reps					

CARDIO WORKOUT

Exercise	Duration	Pace	Heart Rate	Calories

WATER 1 cup per circle
(1 cup = 8 ounces ~ 240ml) ○○○○○○○○○○○○○○○○○

DATE: | **WEEK:** | **WEIGHT:**

Warm Up/ Stretching   **Duration:**

Exercise		Set 1	Set 2	Set 3	Set 4	Set 5
	Weight					
	Reps					
	Weight					
	Reps					
	Weight					
	Reps					
	Weight					
	Reps					
	Weight					
	Reps					
	Weight					
	Reps					
	Weight					
	Reps					
	Weight					
	Reps					
	Weight					
	Reps					
	Weight					
	Reps					
	Weight					
	Reps					
	Weight					
	Reps					

CARDIO WORKOUT

Exercise	Duration	Pace	Heart Rate	Calories

WATER   1 cup per circle
(1 cup = 8 ounces ~ 240ml)   ○ ○ ○ ○ ○ ○ ○ ○ ○ ○ ○ ○ ○ ○ ○ ○

DATE:		WEEK:		WEIGHT:	

Warm Up/ Stretching	Duration:

Exercise		Set 1	Set 2	Set 3	Set 4	Set 5
	Weight					
	Reps					
	Weight					
	Reps					
	Weight					
	Reps					
	Weight					
	Reps					
	Weight					
	Reps					
	Weight					
	Reps					
	Weight					
	Reps					
	Weight					
	Reps					
	Weight					
	Reps					
	Weight					
	Reps					
	Weight					
	Reps					
	Weight					
	Reps					

CARDIO WORKOUT

Exercise	Duration	Pace	Heart Rate	Calories

WATER   1 cup per circle
(1 cup = 8 ounces ~ 240ml)   ○○○○○○○○○○○○○○○○○

DATE:		WEEK:		WEIGHT:	

Warm Up/ Stretching   **Duration:** | |

Exercise		Set 1	Set 2	Set 3	Set 4	Set 5
	Weight					
	Reps					
	Weight					
	Reps					
	Weight					
	Reps					
	Weight					
	Reps					
	Weight					
	Reps					
	Weight					
	Reps					
	Weight					
	Reps					
	Weight					
	Reps					
	Weight					
	Reps					
	Weight					
	Reps					
	Weight					
	Reps					
	Weight					
	Reps					

CARDIO WORKOUT

Exercise	Duration	Pace	Heart Rate	Calories

WATER   **1 cup per circle**
(1 cup = 8 ounces ~ 240ml)   ○○○○○○○○○○○○○○○○○

DATE:		WEEK:		WEIGHT:	

Warm Up/ Stretching		Duration:	

Exercise		Set 1	Set 2	Set 3	Set 4	Set 5
	Weight					
	Reps					
	Weight					
	Reps					
	Weight					
	Reps					
	Weight					
	Reps					
	Weight					
	Reps					
	Weight					
	Reps					
	Weight					
	Reps					
	Weight					
	Reps					
	Weight					
	Reps					
	Weight					
	Reps					
	Weight					
	Reps					
	Weight					
	Reps					

CARDIO WORKOUT

Exercise	Duration	Pace	Heart Rate	Calories

WATER   1 cup per circle
(1 cup = 8 ounces ~ 240ml)   ○ ○ ○ ○ ○ ○ ○ ○ ○ ○ ○ ○ ○ ○ ○

DATE:		WEEK:		WEIGHT:	

Warm Up/ Stretching   Duration:

Exercise		Set 1	Set 2	Set 3	Set 4	Set 5
	Weight					
	Reps					
	Weight					
	Reps					
	Weight					
	Reps					
	Weight					
	Reps					
	Weight					
	Reps					
	Weight					
	Reps					
	Weight					
	Reps					
	Weight					
	Reps					
	Weight					
	Reps					
	Weight					
	Reps					
	Weight					
	Reps					
	Weight					
	Reps					

CARDIO WORKOUT

Exercise	Duration	Pace	Heart Rate	Calories

WATER   1 cup per circle
(1 cup = 8 ounces ~ 240ml)   ○○○○○○○○○○○○○○○○○

DATE:		WEEK:		WEIGHT:	

Warm Up/ Stretching Duration: [ ]

Exercise		Set 1	Set 2	Set 3	Set 4	Set 5
	Weight					
	Reps					
	Weight					
	Reps					
	Weight					
	Reps					
	Weight					
	Reps					
	Weight					
	Reps					
	Weight					
	Reps					
	Weight					
	Reps					
	Weight					
	Reps					
	Weight					
	Reps					
	Weight					
	Reps					
	Weight					
	Reps					
	Weight					
	Reps					

CARDIO WORKOUT

Exercise	Duration	Pace	Heart Rate	Calories

WATER   1 cup per circle
(1 cup = 8 ounces ~ 240ml)   ○○○○○○○○○○○○○○○○○○

DATE:	WEEK:	WEIGHT:

Warm Up/ Stretching　　　　　　　　　　　　　　　**Duration:**

Exercise		Set 1	Set 2	Set 3	Set 4	Set 5
	Weight					
	Reps					
	Weight					
	Reps					
	Weight					
	Reps					
	Weight					
	Reps					
	Weight					
	Reps					
	Weight					
	Reps					
	Weight					
	Reps					
	Weight					
	Reps					
	Weight					
	Reps					
	Weight					
	Reps					
	Weight					
	Reps					
	Weight					
	Reps					

CARDIO WORKOUT

Exercise	Duration	Pace	Heart Rate	Calories

WATER   1 cup per circle
(1 cup = 8 ounces ~ 240ml)   ○ ○ ○ ○ ○ ○ ○ ○ ○ ○ ○ ○ ○ ○ ○ ○

DATE:		WEEK:		WEIGHT:	

Warm Up/ Stretching　　　　　　　　　　　　Duration:

Exercise		Set 1	Set 2	Set 3	Set 4	Set 5
	Weight					
	Reps					
	Weight					
	Reps					
	Weight					
	Reps					
	Weight					
	Reps					
	Weight					
	Reps					
	Weight					
	Reps					
	Weight					
	Reps					
	Weight					
	Reps					
	Weight					
	Reps					
	Weight					
	Reps					
	Weight					
	Reps					
	Weight					
	Reps					

CARDIO WORKOUT

Exercise	Duration	Pace	Heart Rate	Calories

WATER   1 cup per circle
(1 cup = 8 ounces ~ 240ml)   ◯ ◯ ◯ ◯ ◯ ◯ ◯ ◯ ◯ ◯ ◯ ◯ ◯ ◯ ◯

DATE:		WEEK:		WEIGHT:	

Warm Up/ Stretching   Duration: [ ]

Exercise		Set 1	Set 2	Set 3	Set 4	Set 5
	Weight					
	Reps					
	Weight					
	Reps					
	Weight					
	Reps					
	Weight					
	Reps					
	Weight					
	Reps					
	Weight					
	Reps					
	Weight					
	Reps					
	Weight					
	Reps					
	Weight					
	Reps					
	Weight					
	Reps					
	Weight					
	Reps					
	Weight					
	Reps					
	Weight					
	Reps					

CARDIO WORKOUT

Exercise	Duration	Pace	Heart Rate	Calories

WATER   1 cup per circle
(1 cup = 8 ounces ~ 240ml)   ○○○○○○○○○○○○○○○○○

DATE: [   ]   **WEEK:** [   ]   **WEIGHT:** [   ]

| Warm Up/ Stretching | | | | **Duration:** | | [   ] |

Exercise		Set 1	Set 2	Set 3	Set 4	Set 5
	Weight					
	Reps					
	Weight					
	Reps					
	Weight					
	Reps					
	Weight					
	Reps					
	Weight					
	Reps					
	Weight					
	Reps					
	Weight					
	Reps					
	Weight					
	Reps					
	Weight					
	Reps					
	Weight					
	Reps					
	Weight					
	Reps					
	Weight					
	Reps					
	Weight					
	Reps					

CARDIO WORKOUT

Exercise	Duration	Pace	Heart Rate	Calories

WATER   1 cup per circle
(1 cup = 8 ounces ~ 240ml)   ○○○○○○○○○○○○○○○○

DATE:	WEEK:	WEIGHT:

Warm Up/ Stretching Duration:

Exercise		Set 1	Set 2	Set 3	Set 4	Set 5
	Weight					
	Reps					
	Weight					
	Reps					
	Weight					
	Reps					
	Weight					
	Reps					
	Weight					
	Reps					
	Weight					
	Reps					
	Weight					
	Reps					
	Weight					
	Reps					
	Weight					
	Reps					
	Weight					
	Reps					
	Weight					
	Reps					
	Weight					
	Reps					

CARDIO WORKOUT

Exercise	Duration	Pace	Heart Rate	Calories

WATER   1 cup per circle
(1 cup = 8 ounces ~ 240ml)   ○ ○ ○ ○ ○ ○ ○ ○ ○ ○ ○ ○ ○ ○ ○ ○

DATE:		WEEK:		WEIGHT:	

Warm Up/ Stretching Duration:

Exercise		Set 1	Set 2	Set 3	Set 4	Set 5
	Weight					
	Reps					
	Weight					
	Reps					
	Weight					
	Reps					
	Weight					
	Reps					
	Weight					
	Reps					
	Weight					
	Reps					
	Weight					
	Reps					
	Weight					
	Reps					
	Weight					
	Reps					
	Weight					
	Reps					
	Weight					
	Reps					
	Weight					
	Reps					

CARDIO WORKOUT

Exercise	Duration	Pace	Heart Rate	Calories

WATER   1 cup per circle
(1 cup = 8 ounces ~ 240ml)   ○ ○ ○ ○ ○ ○ ○ ○ ○ ○ ○ ○ ○ ○ ○ ○

DATE:	WEEK:	WEIGHT:

Warm Up/ Stretching   **Duration:**

Exercise		Set 1	Set 2	Set 3	Set 4	Set 5
	Weight					
	Reps					
	Weight					
	Reps					
	Weight					
	Reps					
	Weight					
	Reps					
	Weight					
	Reps					
	Weight					
	Reps					
	Weight					
	Reps					
	Weight					
	Reps					
	Weight					
	Reps					
	Weight					
	Reps					
	Weight					
	Reps					
	Weight					
	Reps					

CARDIO WORKOUT

Exercise	Duration	Pace	Heart Rate	Calories

WATER   1 cup per circle
(1 cup = 8 ounces ~ 240ml)   ○ ○ ○ ○ ○ ○ ○ ○ ○ ○ ○ ○ ○ ○ ○ ○

DATE:		WEEK:		WEIGHT:	

Warm Up/ Stretching					Duration:	

Exercise		Set 1	Set 2	Set 3	Set 4	Set 5
	Weight					
	Reps					
	Weight					
	Reps					
	Weight					
	Reps					
	Weight					
	Reps					
	Weight					
	Reps					
	Weight					
	Reps					
	Weight					
	Reps					
	Weight					
	Reps					
	Weight					
	Reps					
	Weight					
	Reps					
	Weight					
	Reps					
	Weight					
	Reps					
	Weight					
	Reps					

CARDIO WORKOUT

Exercise	Duration	Pace	Heart Rate	Calories

WATER   1 cup per circle
(1 cup = 8 ounces ~ 240ml)   ○○○○○○○○○○○○○○○○

DATE: _____ **WEEK:** _____ **WEIGHT:** _____

Warm Up/ Stretching		Duration: _____

Exercise		Set 1	Set 2	Set 3	Set 4	Set 5
	Weight					
	Reps					
	Weight					
	Reps					
	Weight					
	Reps					
	Weight					
	Reps					
	Weight					
	Reps					
	Weight					
	Reps					
	Weight					
	Reps					
	Weight					
	Reps					
	Weight					
	Reps					
	Weight					
	Reps					
	Weight					
	Reps					
	Weight					
	Reps					

CARDIO WORKOUT

Exercise	Duration	Pace	Heart Rate	Calories

WATER   1 cup per circle
(1 cup = 8 ounces ~ 240ml)   ○○○○○○○○○○○○○○○○○○

DATE:		WEEK:		WEIGHT:	

Warm Up/ Stretching		Duration:	

Exercise		Set 1	Set 2	Set 3	Set 4	Set 5
	Weight					
	Reps					
	Weight					
	Reps					
	Weight					
	Reps					
	Weight					
	Reps					
	Weight					
	Reps					
	Weight					
	Reps					
	Weight					
	Reps					
	Weight					
	Reps					
	Weight					
	Reps					
	Weight					
	Reps					
	Weight					
	Reps					
	Weight					
	Reps					
	Weight					
	Reps					

CARDIO WORKOUT

Exercise	Duration	Pace	Heart Rate	Calories

WATER   1 cup per circle
(1 cup = 8 ounces ~ 240ml)   ○ ○ ○ ○ ○ ○ ○ ○ ○ ○ ○ ○ ○ ○ ○

DATE:		WEEK:		WEIGHT:	

Warm Up/ Stretching Duration: [   ]

Exercise		Set 1	Set 2	Set 3	Set 4	Set 5
	Weight					
	Reps					
	Weight					
	Reps					
	Weight					
	Reps					
	Weight					
	Reps					
	Weight					
	Reps					
	Weight					
	Reps					
	Weight					
	Reps					
	Weight					
	Reps					
	Weight					
	Reps					
	Weight					
	Reps					
	Weight					
	Reps					
	Weight					
	Reps					

CARDIO WORKOUT

Exercise	Duration	Pace	Heart Rate	Calories

WATER   1 cup per circle
(1 cup = 8 ounces ~ 240ml)   ○○○○○○○○○○○○○○○○○○

DATE:		WEEK:		WEIGHT:	

Warm Up/ Stretching	Duration:	

Exercise		Set 1	Set 2	Set 3	Set 4	Set 5
	Weight					
	Reps					
	Weight					
	Reps					
	Weight					
	Reps					
	Weight					
	Reps					
	Weight					
	Reps					
	Weight					
	Reps					
	Weight					
	Reps					
	Weight					
	Reps					
	Weight					
	Reps					
	Weight					
	Reps					
	Weight					
	Reps					
	Weight					
	Reps					
	Weight					
	Reps					

CARDIO WORKOUT

Exercise	Duration	Pace	Heart Rate	Calories

WATER   1 cup per circle
(1 cup = 8 ounces ~ 240ml)   ○○○○○○○○○○○○○○○○○

DATE:	WEEK:	WEIGHT:

Warm Up/ Stretching   Duration:

Exercise		Set 1	Set 2	Set 3	Set 4	Set 5
	Weight					
	Reps					
	Weight					
	Reps					
	Weight					
	Reps					
	Weight					
	Reps					
	Weight					
	Reps					
	Weight					
	Reps					
	Weight					
	Reps					
	Weight					
	Reps					
	Weight					
	Reps					
	Weight					
	Reps					
	Weight					
	Reps					
	Weight					
	Reps					

CARDIO WORKOUT

Exercise	Duration	Pace	Heart Rate	Calories

WATER   1 cup per circle
(1 cup = 8 ounces ~ 240ml)   ○○○○○○○○○○○○○○○○

DATE:		WEEK:		WEIGHT:	

Warm Up/ Stretching   Duration: [ ]

Exercise		Set 1	Set 2	Set 3	Set 4	Set 5
	Weight					
	Reps					
	Weight					
	Reps					
	Weight					
	Reps					
	Weight					
	Reps					
	Weight					
	Reps					
	Weight					
	Reps					
	Weight					
	Reps					
	Weight					
	Reps					
	Weight					
	Reps					
	Weight					
	Reps					
	Weight					
	Reps					
	Weight					
	Reps					
	Weight					
	Reps					

CARDIO WORKOUT

Exercise	Duration	Pace	Heart Rate	Calories

WATER   1 cup per circle
(1 cup = 8 ounces ~ 240ml)   ○○○○○○○○○○○○○○○○○

DATE: | **WEEK:** | **WEIGHT:**

Warm Up/ Stretching   Duration:

Exercise		Set 1	Set 2	Set 3	Set 4	Set 5
	Weight					
	Reps					
	Weight					
	Reps					
	Weight					
	Reps					
	Weight					
	Reps					
	Weight					
	Reps					
	Weight					
	Reps					
	Weight					
	Reps					
	Weight					
	Reps					
	Weight					
	Reps					
	Weight					
	Reps					
	Weight					
	Reps					
	Weight					
	Reps					

CARDIO WORKOUT

Exercise	Duration	Pace	Heart Rate	Calories

WATER   1 cup per circle
(1 cup = 8 ounces ~ 240ml)   ○○○○○○○○○○○○○○○○○

DATE:	WEEK:	WEIGHT:

Warm Up/ Stretching	Duration:

Exercise		Set 1	Set 2	Set 3	Set 4	Set 5
	Weight					
	Reps					
	Weight					
	Reps					
	Weight					
	Reps					
	Weight					
	Reps					
	Weight					
	Reps					
	Weight					
	Reps					
	Weight					
	Reps					
	Weight					
	Reps					
	Weight					
	Reps					
	Weight					
	Reps					
	Weight					
	Reps					
	Weight					
	Reps					

CARDIO WORKOUT

Exercise	Duration	Pace	Heart Rate	Calories

WATER   1 cup per circle
(1 cup = 8 ounces ~ 240ml)   ○○○○○○○○○○○○○○○

DATE:	WEEK:	WEIGHT:

Warm Up/ Stretching   Duration:

Exercise		Set 1	Set 2	Set 3	Set 4	Set 5
	Weight					
	Reps					
	Weight					
	Reps					
	Weight					
	Reps					
	Weight					
	Reps					
	Weight					
	Reps					
	Weight					
	Reps					
	Weight					
	Reps					
	Weight					
	Reps					
	Weight					
	Reps					
	Weight					
	Reps					
	Weight					
	Reps					
	Weight					
	Reps					

CARDIO WORKOUT

Exercise	Duration	Pace	Heart Rate	Calories

WATER   1 cup per circle
(1 cup = 8 ounces ~ 240ml)   ○○○○○○○○○○○○○○○○○

DATE:	WEEK:	WEIGHT:

Warm Up/ Stretching   **Duration:**

Exercise		Set 1	Set 2	Set 3	Set 4	Set 5
	Weight					
	Reps					
	Weight					
	Reps					
	Weight					
	Reps					
	Weight					
	Reps					
	Weight					
	Reps					
	Weight					
	Reps					
	Weight					
	Reps					
	Weight					
	Reps					
	Weight					
	Reps					
	Weight					
	Reps					
	Weight					
	Reps					
	Weight					
	Reps					
	Weight					
	Reps					

CARDIO WORKOUT

Exercise	Duration	Pace	Heart Rate	Calories

WATER   1 cup per circle
(1 cup = 8 ounces ~ 240ml)   ○○○○○○○○○○○○○○○○○

DATE:		WEEK:		WEIGHT:	

Warm Up/ Stretching   Duration: [   ]

Exercise		Set 1	Set 2	Set 3	Set 4	Set 5
	Weight					
	Reps					
	Weight					
	Reps					
	Weight					
	Reps					
	Weight					
	Reps					
	Weight					
	Reps					
	Weight					
	Reps					
	Weight					
	Reps					
	Weight					
	Reps					
	Weight					
	Reps					
	Weight					
	Reps					
	Weight					
	Reps					
	Weight					
	Reps					

CARDIO WORKOUT

Exercise	Duration	Pace	Heart Rate	Calories

WATER   1 cup per circle
(1 cup = 8 ounces ~ 240ml)   ○○○○○○○○○○○○○○○○○

DATE: [   ] **WEEK:** [   ] **WEIGHT:** [   ]

Warm Up/ Stretching						Duration: [ ]

Exercise		Set 1	Set 2	Set 3	Set 4	Set 5
	Weight					
	Reps					
	Weight					
	Reps					
	Weight					
	Reps					
	Weight					
	Reps					
	Weight					
	Reps					
	Weight					
	Reps					
	Weight					
	Reps					
	Weight					
	Reps					
	Weight					
	Reps					
	Weight					
	Reps					
	Weight					
	Reps					
	Weight					
	Reps					
	Weight					
	Reps					

CARDIO WORKOUT

Exercise	Duration	Pace	Heart Rate	Calories

WATER   1 cup per circle
(1 cup = 8 ounces ~ 240ml)   ○○○○○○○○○○○○○○○○○

DATE: | **WEEK:** | **WEIGHT:**

Warm Up/ Stretching **Duration:**

Exercise		Set 1	Set 2	Set 3	Set 4	Set 5
	Weight					
	Reps					
	Weight					
	Reps					
	Weight					
	Reps					
	Weight					
	Reps					
	Weight					
	Reps					
	Weight					
	Reps					
	Weight					
	Reps					
	Weight					
	Reps					
	Weight					
	Reps					
	Weight					
	Reps					
	Weight					
	Reps					
	Weight					
	Reps					

CARDIO WORKOUT

Exercise	Duration	Pace	Heart Rate	Calories

WATER   1 cup per circle
(1 cup = 8 ounces ~ 240ml)   ○ ○ ○ ○ ○ ○ ○ ○ ○ ○ ○ ○ ○ ○ ○ ○

DATE:	WEEK:	WEIGHT:

Warm Up/ Stretching					Duration:	

Exercise		Set 1	Set 2	Set 3	Set 4	Set 5
	Weight					
	Reps					
	Weight					
	Reps					
	Weight					
	Reps					
	Weight					
	Reps					
	Weight					
	Reps					
	Weight					
	Reps					
	Weight					
	Reps					
	Weight					
	Reps					
	Weight					
	Reps					
	Weight					
	Reps					
	Weight					
	Reps					
	Weight					
	Reps					

CARDIO WORKOUT

Exercise	Duration	Pace	Heart Rate	Calories

WATER   1 cup per circle
(1 cup = 8 ounces ~ 240ml)   ○○○○○○○○○○○○○○○○

DATE: [ ] **WEEK:** [ ] **WEIGHT:** [ ]

Warm Up/ Stretching   Duration: [ ]

Exercise		Set 1	Set 2	Set 3	Set 4	Set 5
	Weight					
	Reps					
	Weight					
	Reps					
	Weight					
	Reps					
	Weight					
	Reps					
	Weight					
	Reps					
	Weight					
	Reps					
	Weight					
	Reps					
	Weight					
	Reps					
	Weight					
	Reps					
	Weight					
	Reps					
	Weight					
	Reps					
	Weight					
	Reps					
	Weight					
	Reps					

CARDIO WORKOUT

Exercise	Duration	Pace	Heart Rate	Calories

WATER 1 cup per circle
(1 cup = 8 ounces ~ 240ml)   ○ ○ ○ ○ ○ ○ ○ ○ ○ ○ ○ ○ ○ ○ ○ ○

DATE:		WEEK:		WEIGHT:	

Warm Up/ Stretching   **Duration:** [ ]

Exercise		Set 1	Set 2	Set 3	Set 4	Set 5
	Weight					
	Reps					
	Weight					
	Reps					
	Weight					
	Reps					
	Weight					
	Reps					
	Weight					
	Reps					
	Weight					
	Reps					
	Weight					
	Reps					
	Weight					
	Reps					
	Weight					
	Reps					
	Weight					
	Reps					
	Weight					
	Reps					
	Weight					
	Reps					

CARDIO WORKOUT

Exercise	Duration	Pace	Heart Rate	Calories

WATER   1 cup per circle
(1 cup = 8 ounces ~ 240ml)   ○○○○○○○○○○○○○○○

DATE:	WEEK:	WEIGHT:

Warm Up/ Stretching Duration:

Exercise		Set 1	Set 2	Set 3	Set 4	Set 5
	Weight					
	Reps					
	Weight					
	Reps					
	Weight					
	Reps					
	Weight					
	Reps					
	Weight					
	Reps					
	Weight					
	Reps					
	Weight					
	Reps					
	Weight					
	Reps					
	Weight					
	Reps					
	Weight					
	Reps					
	Weight					
	Reps					
	Weight					
	Reps					

CARDIO WORKOUT

Exercise	Duration	Pace	Heart Rate	Calories

WATER   1 cup per circle
(1 cup = 8 ounces ~ 240ml)   ○○○○○○○○○○○○○○○○○○

DATE:	WEEK:	WEIGHT:

Warm Up/ Stretching   Duration:

Exercise		Set 1	Set 2	Set 3	Set 4	Set 5
	Weight					
	Reps					
	Weight					
	Reps					
	Weight					
	Reps					
	Weight					
	Reps					
	Weight					
	Reps					
	Weight					
	Reps					
	Weight					
	Reps					
	Weight					
	Reps					
	Weight					
	Reps					
	Weight					
	Reps					
	Weight					
	Reps					
	Weight					
	Reps					
	Weight					
	Reps					

CARDIO WORKOUT

Exercise	Duration	Pace	Heart Rate	Calories

WATER   1 cup per circle
(1 cup = 8 ounces ~ 240ml)   ○○○○○○○○○○○○○○○○○

DATE: [   ]　　**WEEK:** [   ]　　**WEIGHT:** [   ]

Warm Up/ Stretching　　　　　　　　　**Duration:** [   ]

Exercise		Set 1	Set 2	Set 3	Set 4	Set 5
	Weight					
	Reps					
	Weight					
	Reps					
	Weight					
	Reps					
	Weight					
	Reps					
	Weight					
	Reps					
	Weight					
	Reps					
	Weight					
	Reps					
	Weight					
	Reps					
	Weight					
	Reps					
	Weight					
	Reps					
	Weight					
	Reps					
	Weight					
	Reps					

CARDIO WORKOUT

Exercise	Duration	Pace	Heart Rate	Calories

WATER　1 cup per circle
(1 cup = 8 ounces ~ 240ml)　　○○○○○○○○○○○○○○○○

DATE:		WEEK:		WEIGHT:	

Warm Up/ Stretching	Duration:

Exercise		Set 1	Set 2	Set 3	Set 4	Set 5
	Weight					
	Reps					
	Weight					
	Reps					
	Weight					
	Reps					
	Weight					
	Reps					
	Weight					
	Reps					
	Weight					
	Reps					
	Weight					
	Reps					
	Weight					
	Reps					
	Weight					
	Reps					
	Weight					
	Reps					
	Weight					
	Reps					
	Weight					
	Reps					

CARDIO WORKOUT

Exercise	Duration	Pace	Heart Rate	Calories

WATER   1 cup per circle
(1 cup = 8 ounces ~ 240ml)   ○○○○○○○○○○○○○○○○○○

DATE:	WEEK:	WEIGHT:

Warm Up/ Stretching	Duration:

Exercise		Set 1	Set 2	Set 3	Set 4	Set 5
	Weight					
	Reps					
	Weight					
	Reps					
	Weight					
	Reps					
	Weight					
	Reps					
	Weight					
	Reps					
	Weight					
	Reps					
	Weight					
	Reps					
	Weight					
	Reps					
	Weight					
	Reps					
	Weight					
	Reps					
	Weight					
	Reps					

CARDIO WORKOUT

Exercise	Duration	Pace	Heart Rate	Calories

WATER   1 cup per circle
(1 cup = 8 ounces ~ 240ml)   ○ ○ ○ ○ ○ ○ ○ ○ ○ ○ ○ ○ ○ ○ ○ ○

DATE:	WEEK:	WEIGHT:

Warm Up/ Stretching	Duration:

Exercise		Set 1	Set 2	Set 3	Set 4	Set 5
	Weight					
	Reps					
	Weight					
	Reps					
	Weight					
	Reps					
	Weight					
	Reps					
	Weight					
	Reps					
	Weight					
	Reps					
	Weight					
	Reps					
	Weight					
	Reps					
	Weight					
	Reps					
	Weight					
	Reps					
	Weight					
	Reps					
	Weight					
	Reps					

CARDIO WORKOUT

Exercise	Duration	Pace	Heart Rate	Calories

WATER   1 cup per circle
(1 cup = 8 ounces ~ 240ml)   ○○○○○○○○○○○○○○○○

DATE: _____   **WEEK:** _____   **WEIGHT:** _____

Warm Up/ Stretching   **Duration:** _____

Exercise		Set 1	Set 2	Set 3	Set 4	Set 5
	Weight					
	Reps					
	Weight					
	Reps					
	Weight					
	Reps					
	Weight					
	Reps					
	Weight					
	Reps					
	Weight					
	Reps					
	Weight					
	Reps					
	Weight					
	Reps					
	Weight					
	Reps					
	Weight					
	Reps					
	Weight					
	Reps					
	Weight					
	Reps					

CARDIO WORKOUT

Exercise	Duration	Pace	Heart Rate	Calories

WATER   1 cup per circle
(1 cup = 8 ounces ~ 240ml)   ○○○○○○○○○○○○○○○○

DATE:		WEEK:		WEIGHT:	

Warm Up/ Stretching			Duration:	

Exercise		Set 1	Set 2	Set 3	Set 4	Set 5
	Weight					
	Reps					
	Weight					
	Reps					
	Weight					
	Reps					
	Weight					
	Reps					
	Weight					
	Reps					
	Weight					
	Reps					
	Weight					
	Reps					
	Weight					
	Reps					
	Weight					
	Reps					
	Weight					
	Reps					
	Weight					
	Reps					
	Weight					
	Reps					

CARDIO WORKOUT

Exercise	Duration	Pace	Heart Rate	Calories

WATER   1 cup per circle
(1 cup = 8 ounces ~ 240ml)   ○ ○ ○ ○ ○ ○ ○ ○ ○ ○ ○ ○ ○ ○ ○

DATE:		WEEK:		WEIGHT:	

Warm Up/ Stretching   Duration:

Exercise		Set 1	Set 2	Set 3	Set 4	Set 5
	Weight					
	Reps					
	Weight					
	Reps					
	Weight					
	Reps					
	Weight					
	Reps					
	Weight					
	Reps					
	Weight					
	Reps					
	Weight					
	Reps					
	Weight					
	Reps					
	Weight					
	Reps					
	Weight					
	Reps					
	Weight					
	Reps					
	Weight					
	Reps					

CARDIO WORKOUT

Exercise	Duration	Pace	Heart Rate	Calories

WATER   1 cup per circle
(1 cup = 8 ounces ~ 240ml)   ○ ○ ○ ○ ○ ○ ○ ○ ○ ○ ○ ○ ○ ○ ○

DATE:	WEEK:	WEIGHT:

Warm Up/ Stretching   **Duration:**

Exercise		Set 1	Set 2	Set 3	Set 4	Set 5
	Weight					
	Reps					
	Weight					
	Reps					
	Weight					
	Reps					
	Weight					
	Reps					
	Weight					
	Reps					
	Weight					
	Reps					
	Weight					
	Reps					
	Weight					
	Reps					
	Weight					
	Reps					
	Weight					
	Reps					
	Weight					
	Reps					
	Weight					
	Reps					

CARDIO WORKOUT

Exercise	Duration	Pace	Heart Rate	Calories

WATER   1 cup per circle
(1 cup = 8 ounces ~ 240ml)   ○○○○○○○○○○○○○○○○

DATE: [ ]   **WEEK:** [ ]   **WEIGHT:** [ ]

Warm Up/ Stretching   Duration: [ ]

Exercise		Set 1	Set 2	Set 3	Set 4	Set 5
	Weight					
	Reps					
	Weight					
	Reps					
	Weight					
	Reps					
	Weight					
	Reps					
	Weight					
	Reps					
	Weight					
	Reps					
	Weight					
	Reps					
	Weight					
	Reps					
	Weight					
	Reps					
	Weight					
	Reps					
	Weight					
	Reps					
	Weight					
	Reps					

CARDIO WORKOUT

Exercise	Duration	Pace	Heart Rate	Calories

WATER   1 cup per circle
(1 cup = 8 ounces ~ 240ml)   ○○○○○○○○○○○○○○○○

DATE:	WEEK:	WEIGHT:

Warm Up/ Stretching		Duration:	

Exercise		Set 1	Set 2	Set 3	Set 4	Set 5
	Weight					
	Reps					
	Weight					
	Reps					
	Weight					
	Reps					
	Weight					
	Reps					
	Weight					
	Reps					
	Weight					
	Reps					
	Weight					
	Reps					
	Weight					
	Reps					
	Weight					
	Reps					
	Weight					
	Reps					
	Weight					
	Reps					
	Weight					
	Reps					
	Weight					
	Reps					

CARDIO WORKOUT

Exercise	Duration	Pace	Heart Rate	Calories

WATER   1 cup per circle
(1 cup = 8 ounces ~ 240ml)   ○○○○○○○○○○○○○○○

DATE:	WEEK:	WEIGHT:

Warm Up/ Stretching   Duration: [ ]

Exercise		Set 1	Set 2	Set 3	Set 4	Set 5
	Weight					
	Reps					
	Weight					
	Reps					
	Weight					
	Reps					
	Weight					
	Reps					
	Weight					
	Reps					
	Weight					
	Reps					
	Weight					
	Reps					
	Weight					
	Reps					
	Weight					
	Reps					
	Weight					
	Reps					
	Weight					
	Reps					

CARDIO WORKOUT

Exercise	Duration	Pace	Heart Rate	Calories

WATER   1 cup per circle
(1 cup = 8 ounces ~ 240ml)   ○ ○ ○ ○ ○ ○ ○ ○ ○ ○ ○ ○ ○ ○ ○ ○

DATE:		WEEK:		WEIGHT:	

Warm Up/ Stretching						Duration:	

Exercise		Set 1	Set 2	Set 3	Set 4	Set 5
	Weight					
	Reps					
	Weight					
	Reps					
	Weight					
	Reps					
	Weight					
	Reps					
	Weight					
	Reps					
	Weight					
	Reps					
	Weight					
	Reps					
	Weight					
	Reps					
	Weight					
	Reps					
	Weight					
	Reps					
	Weight					
	Reps					
	Weight					
	Reps					

CARDIO WORKOUT

Exercise	Duration	Pace	Heart Rate	Calories

WATER   1 cup per circle
(1 cup = 8 ounces ~ 240ml)   ○ ○ ○ ○ ○ ○ ○ ○ ○ ○ ○ ○ ○ ○ ○

DATE:	WEEK:	WEIGHT:

Warm Up/ Stretching   **Duration:**

Exercise		Set 1	Set 2	Set 3	Set 4	Set 5
	Weight					
	Reps					
	Weight					
	Reps					
	Weight					
	Reps					
	Weight					
	Reps					
	Weight					
	Reps					
	Weight					
	Reps					
	Weight					
	Reps					
	Weight					
	Reps					
	Weight					
	Reps					
	Weight					
	Reps					
	Weight					
	Reps					
	Weight					
	Reps					

CARDIO WORKOUT

Exercise	Duration	Pace	Heart Rate	Calories

WATER   1 cup per circle
(1 cup = 8 ounces ~ 240ml)   ○○○○○○○○○○○○○○○○

DATE:	WEEK:	WEIGHT:

Warm Up/ Stretching	Duration:

Exercise		Set 1	Set 2	Set 3	Set 4	Set 5
	Weight					
	Reps					
	Weight					
	Reps					
	Weight					
	Reps					
	Weight					
	Reps					
	Weight					
	Reps					
	Weight					
	Reps					
	Weight					
	Reps					
	Weight					
	Reps					
	Weight					
	Reps					
	Weight					
	Reps					
	Weight					
	Reps					
	Weight					
	Reps					

CARDIO WORKOUT

Exercise	Duration	Pace	Heart Rate	Calories

WATER   1 cup per circle
(1 cup = 8 ounces ~ 240ml)   ○○○○○○○○○○○○○○○○

DATE:		WEEK:		WEIGHT:	

Warm Up/ Stretching　　　　　　　　　　　**Duration:**

Exercise		Set 1	Set 2	Set 3	Set 4	Set 5
	Weight					
	Reps					
	Weight					
	Reps					
	Weight					
	Reps					
	Weight					
	Reps					
	Weight					
	Reps					
	Weight					
	Reps					
	Weight					
	Reps					
	Weight					
	Reps					
	Weight					
	Reps					
	Weight					
	Reps					
	Weight					
	Reps					
	Weight					
	Reps					

CARDIO WORKOUT

Exercise	Duration	Pace	Heart Rate	Calories

WATER   1 cup per circle
(1 cup = 8 ounces ~ 240ml)   ○○○○○○○○○○○○○○○○○

DATE:		WEEK:		WEIGHT:	

Warm Up/ Stretching				Duration:	

Exercise		Set 1	Set 2	Set 3	Set 4	Set 5
	Weight					
	Reps					
	Weight					
	Reps					
	Weight					
	Reps					
	Weight					
	Reps					
	Weight					
	Reps					
	Weight					
	Reps					
	Weight					
	Reps					
	Weight					
	Reps					
	Weight					
	Reps					
	Weight					
	Reps					
	Weight					
	Reps					
	Weight					
	Reps					
	Weight					
	Reps					

CARDIO WORKOUT

Exercise	Duration	Pace	Heart Rate	Calories

WATER   1 cup per circle
(1 cup = 8 ounces ~ 240ml)   ○○○○○○○○○○○○○○○○

DATE:	WEEK:	WEIGHT:

Warm Up/ Stretching	Duration:

Exercise		Set 1	Set 2	Set 3	Set 4	Set 5
	Weight					
	Reps					
	Weight					
	Reps					
	Weight					
	Reps					
	Weight					
	Reps					
	Weight					
	Reps					
	Weight					
	Reps					
	Weight					
	Reps					
	Weight					
	Reps					
	Weight					
	Reps					
	Weight					
	Reps					
	Weight					
	Reps					
	Weight					
	Reps					

CARDIO WORKOUT

Exercise	Duration	Pace	Heart Rate	Calories

WATER   1 cup per circle
(1 cup = 8 ounces ~ 240ml)   ○○○○○○○○○○○○○○○○

DATE: | **WEEK:** | **WEIGHT:**

| Warm Up/ Stretching | | Duration: | |

Exercise		Set 1	Set 2	Set 3	Set 4	Set 5
	Weight					
	Reps					
	Weight					
	Reps					
	Weight					
	Reps					
	Weight					
	Reps					
	Weight					
	Reps					
	Weight					
	Reps					
	Weight					
	Reps					
	Weight					
	Reps					
	Weight					
	Reps					
	Weight					
	Reps					
	Weight					
	Reps					
	Weight					
	Reps					

CARDIO WORKOUT

Exercise	Duration	Pace	Heart Rate	Calories

WATER   1 cup per circle
(1 cup = 8 ounces ~ 240ml)   ○○○○○○○○○○○○○○○○○○○

DATE:	WEEK:	WEIGHT:

Warm Up/ Stretching   Duration:

Exercise		Set 1	Set 2	Set 3	Set 4	Set 5
	Weight					
	Reps					
	Weight					
	Reps					
	Weight					
	Reps					
	Weight					
	Reps					
	Weight					
	Reps					
	Weight					
	Reps					
	Weight					
	Reps					
	Weight					
	Reps					
	Weight					
	Reps					
	Weight					
	Reps					
	Weight					
	Reps					
	Weight					
	Reps					

CARDIO WORKOUT

Exercise	Duration	Pace	Heart Rate	Calories

WATER   1 cup per circle
(1 cup = 8 ounces ~ 240ml)   ○○○○○○○○○○○○○○○○

DATE:	WEEK:	WEIGHT:

Warm Up/ Stretching Duration:

Exercise		Set 1	Set 2	Set 3	Set 4	Set 5
	Weight					
	Reps					
	Weight					
	Reps					
	Weight					
	Reps					
	Weight					
	Reps					
	Weight					
	Reps					
	Weight					
	Reps					
	Weight					
	Reps					
	Weight					
	Reps					
	Weight					
	Reps					
	Weight					
	Reps					
	Weight					
	Reps					
	Weight					
	Reps					

CARDIO WORKOUT

Exercise	Duration	Pace	Heart Rate	Calories

WATER   1 cup per circle
(1 cup = 8 ounces ~ 240ml)   ○○○○○○○○○○○○○○○○

DATE: | **WEEK:** | **WEIGHT:**

Warm Up/ Stretching **Duration:**

Exercise		Set 1	Set 2	Set 3	Set 4	Set 5
	Weight					
	Reps					
	Weight					
	Reps					
	Weight					
	Reps					
	Weight					
	Reps					
	Weight					
	Reps					
	Weight					
	Reps					
	Weight					
	Reps					
	Weight					
	Reps					
	Weight					
	Reps					
	Weight					
	Reps					
	Weight					
	Reps					
	Weight					
	Reps					

CARDIO WORKOUT

Exercise	Duration	Pace	Heart Rate	Calories

WATER   1 cup per circle
(1 cup = 8 ounces ~ 240ml)   ○○○○○○○○○○○○○○○○○

DATE:	WEEK:	WEIGHT:

Warm Up/ Stretching	Duration:

Exercise		Set 1	Set 2	Set 3	Set 4	Set 5
	Weight					
	Reps					
	Weight					
	Reps					
	Weight					
	Reps					
	Weight					
	Reps					
	Weight					
	Reps					
	Weight					
	Reps					
	Weight					
	Reps					
	Weight					
	Reps					
	Weight					
	Reps					
	Weight					
	Reps					
	Weight					
	Reps					
	Weight					
	Reps					

CARDIO WORKOUT

Exercise	Duration	Pace	Heart Rate	Calories

WATER   1 cup per circle
(1 cup = 8 ounces ~ 240ml)   ○○○○○○○○○○○○○○○○

DATE:		WEEK:		WEIGHT:	

Warm Up/ Stretching Duration: [   ]

Exercise		Set 1	Set 2	Set 3	Set 4	Set 5
	Weight					
	Reps					
	Weight					
	Reps					
	Weight					
	Reps					
	Weight					
	Reps					
	Weight					
	Reps					
	Weight					
	Reps					
	Weight					
	Reps					
	Weight					
	Reps					
	Weight					
	Reps					
	Weight					
	Reps					
	Weight					
	Reps					
	Weight					
	Reps					

CARDIO WORKOUT

Exercise	Duration	Pace	Heart Rate	Calories

WATER   1 cup per circle
(1 cup = 8 ounces ~ 240ml)   ○○○○○○○○○○○○○○○○○○

| DATE: | | WEEK: | | WEIGHT: | |

| Warm Up/ Stretching | | | | | Duration: | |

Exercise		Set 1	Set 2	Set 3	Set 4	Set 5
	Weight					
	Reps					
	Weight					
	Reps					
	Weight					
	Reps					
	Weight					
	Reps					
	Weight					
	Reps					
	Weight					
	Reps					
	Weight					
	Reps					
	Weight					
	Reps					
	Weight					
	Reps					
	Weight					
	Reps					
	Weight					
	Reps					
	Weight					
	Reps					
	Weight					
	Reps					

CARDIO WORKOUT

Exercise	Duration	Pace	Heart Rate	Calories

WATER   1 cup per circle
(1 cup = 8 ounces ~ 240ml)   ○ ○ ○ ○ ○ ○ ○ ○ ○ ○ ○ ○ ○ ○ ○ ○

DATE: | **WEEK:** | **WEIGHT:**

Warm Up/ Stretching **Duration:**

Exercise		Set 1	Set 2	Set 3	Set 4	Set 5
	Weight					
	Reps					
	Weight					
	Reps					
	Weight					
	Reps					
	Weight					
	Reps					
	Weight					
	Reps					
	Weight					
	Reps					
	Weight					
	Reps					
	Weight					
	Reps					
	Weight					
	Reps					
	Weight					
	Reps					
	Weight					
	Reps					
	Weight					
	Reps					

CARDIO WORKOUT

Exercise	Duration	Pace	Heart Rate	Calories

WATER   1 cup per circle
(1 cup = 8 ounces ~ 240ml)   ○○○○○○○○○○○○○○○○○○

DATE:		WEEK:		WEIGHT:	

Warm Up/ Stretching   Duration: [ ]

Exercise		Set 1	Set 2	Set 3	Set 4	Set 5
	Weight					
	Reps					
	Weight					
	Reps					
	Weight					
	Reps					
	Weight					
	Reps					
	Weight					
	Reps					
	Weight					
	Reps					
	Weight					
	Reps					
	Weight					
	Reps					
	Weight					
	Reps					
	Weight					
	Reps					
	Weight					
	Reps					
	Weight					
	Reps					

CARDIO WORKOUT

Exercise	Duration	Pace	Heart Rate	Calories

WATER   1 cup per circle
(1 cup = 8 ounces ~ 240ml)   ○○○○○○○○○○○○○○○

DATE: [   ]   **WEEK:** [   ]   **WEIGHT:** [   ]

Warm Up/ Stretching   **Duration:** [   ]

Exercise		Set 1	Set 2	Set 3	Set 4	Set 5
	Weight					
	Reps					
	Weight					
	Reps					
	Weight					
	Reps					
	Weight					
	Reps					
	Weight					
	Reps					
	Weight					
	Reps					
	Weight					
	Reps					
	Weight					
	Reps					
	Weight					
	Reps					
	Weight					
	Reps					
	Weight					
	Reps					
	Weight					
	Reps					

CARDIO WORKOUT

Exercise	Duration	Pace	Heart Rate	Calories

WATER   1 cup per circle
(1 cup = 8 ounces ~ 240ml)   ○○○○○○○○○○○○○○○○○

DATE:	WEEK:	WEIGHT:

Warm Up/ Stretching				Duration:		

Exercise		Set 1	Set 2	Set 3	Set 4	Set 5
	Weight					
	Reps					
	Weight					
	Reps					
	Weight					
	Reps					
	Weight					
	Reps					
	Weight					
	Reps					
	Weight					
	Reps					
	Weight					
	Reps					
	Weight					
	Reps					
	Weight					
	Reps					
	Weight					
	Reps					
	Weight					
	Reps					
	Weight					
	Reps					

CARDIO WORKOUT

Exercise	Duration	Pace	Heart Rate	Calories

WATER   1 cup per circle
(1 cup = 8 ounces ~ 240ml)   ○○○○○○○○○○○○○○○○

DATE: _____ **WEEK:** _____ **WEIGHT:** _____

Warm Up/ Stretching				**Duration:** _____		

Exercise		Set 1	Set 2	Set 3	Set 4	Set 5
	Weight					
	Reps					
	Weight					
	Reps					
	Weight					
	Reps					
	Weight					
	Reps					
	Weight					
	Reps					
	Weight					
	Reps					
	Weight					
	Reps					
	Weight					
	Reps					
	Weight					
	Reps					
	Weight					
	Reps					
	Weight					
	Reps					
	Weight					
	Reps					

CARDIO WORKOUT

Exercise	Duration	Pace	Heart Rate	Calories

WATER 1 cup per circle
(1 cup = 8 ounces ~ 240ml) ○○○○○○○○○○○○○○○○○

DATE: _____ **WEEK:** _____ **WEIGHT:** _____

Warm Up/ Stretching		**Duration:** _____

Exercise		Set 1	Set 2	Set 3	Set 4	Set 5
	Weight					
	Reps					
	Weight					
	Reps					
	Weight					
	Reps					
	Weight					
	Reps					
	Weight					
	Reps					
	Weight					
	Reps					
	Weight					
	Reps					
	Weight					
	Reps					
	Weight					
	Reps					
	Weight					
	Reps					
	Weight					
	Reps					
	Weight					
	Reps					

CARDIO WORKOUT

Exercise	Duration	Pace	Heart Rate	Calories

WATER   1 cup per circle
(1 cup = 8 ounces ~ 240ml)   ◯◯◯◯◯◯◯◯◯◯◯◯◯◯

DATE:	WEEK:	WEIGHT:

Warm Up/ Stretching   **Duration:**

Exercise		Set 1	Set 2	Set 3	Set 4	Set 5
	Weight					
	Reps					
	Weight					
	Reps					
	Weight					
	Reps					
	Weight					
	Reps					
	Weight					
	Reps					
	Weight					
	Reps					
	Weight					
	Reps					
	Weight					
	Reps					
	Weight					
	Reps					
	Weight					
	Reps					
	Weight					
	Reps					
	Weight					
	Reps					

CARDIO WORKOUT

Exercise	Duration	Pace	Heart Rate	Calories

WATER   1 cup per circle
(1 cup = 8 ounces ~ 240ml)   ○○○○○○○○○○○○○○○○

DATE:	WEEK:	WEIGHT:

Warm Up/ Stretching						Duration:	

Exercise		Set 1	Set 2	Set 3	Set 4	Set 5
	Weight					
	Reps					
	Weight					
	Reps					
	Weight					
	Reps					
	Weight					
	Reps					
	Weight					
	Reps					
	Weight					
	Reps					
	Weight					
	Reps					
	Weight					
	Reps					
	Weight					
	Reps					
	Weight					
	Reps					
	Weight					
	Reps					
	Weight					
	Reps					
	Weight					
	Reps					

CARDIO WORKOUT

Exercise	Duration	Pace	Heart Rate	Calories

WATER   1 cup per circle
(1 cup = 8 ounces ~ 240ml)   ○ ○ ○ ○ ○ ○ ○ ○ ○ ○ ○ ○ ○ ○ ○

DATE:	WEEK:	WEIGHT:

Warm Up/ Stretching   **Duration:**

Exercise		Set 1	Set 2	Set 3	Set 4	Set 5
	Weight					
	Reps					
	Weight					
	Reps					
	Weight					
	Reps					
	Weight					
	Reps					
	Weight					
	Reps					
	Weight					
	Reps					
	Weight					
	Reps					
	Weight					
	Reps					
	Weight					
	Reps					
	Weight					
	Reps					
	Weight					
	Reps					
	Weight					
	Reps					

CARDIO WORKOUT

Exercise	Duration	Pace	Heart Rate	Calories

WATER   1 cup per circle
(1 cup = 8 ounces ~ 240ml)   ○○○○○○○○○○○○○○○○○○

DATE:	WEEK:	WEIGHT:

Warm Up/ Stretching	Duration:

Exercise		Set 1	Set 2	Set 3	Set 4	Set 5
	Weight					
	Reps					
	Weight					
	Reps					
	Weight					
	Reps					
	Weight					
	Reps					
	Weight					
	Reps					
	Weight					
	Reps					
	Weight					
	Reps					
	Weight					
	Reps					
	Weight					
	Reps					
	Weight					
	Reps					
	Weight					
	Reps					
	Weight					
	Reps					

CARDIO WORKOUT

Exercise	Duration	Pace	Heart Rate	Calories

WATER   1 cup per circle
(1 cup = 8 ounces ~ 240ml)   ○○○○○○○○○○○○○○

DATE:		WEEK:		WEIGHT:	

Warm Up/ Stretching Duration: [   ]

Exercise		Set 1	Set 2	Set 3	Set 4	Set 5
	Weight					
	Reps					
	Weight					
	Reps					
	Weight					
	Reps					
	Weight					
	Reps					
	Weight					
	Reps					
	Weight					
	Reps					
	Weight					
	Reps					
	Weight					
	Reps					
	Weight					
	Reps					
	Weight					
	Reps					
	Weight					
	Reps					
	Weight					
	Reps					

CARDIO WORKOUT

Exercise	Duration	Pace	Heart Rate	Calories

WATER   1 cup per circle
(1 cup = 8 ounces ~ 240ml)   ○○○○○○○○○○○○○○○○○

DATE:		WEEK:		WEIGHT:	

Warm Up/ Stretching	Duration:

Exercise		Set 1	Set 2	Set 3	Set 4	Set 5
	Weight					
	Reps					
	Weight					
	Reps					
	Weight					
	Reps					
	Weight					
	Reps					
	Weight					
	Reps					
	Weight					
	Reps					
	Weight					
	Reps					
	Weight					
	Reps					
	Weight					
	Reps					
	Weight					
	Reps					
	Weight					
	Reps					
	Weight					
	Reps					

CARDIO WORKOUT

Exercise	Duration	Pace	Heart Rate	Calories

WATER   1 cup per circle
(1 cup = 8 ounces ~ 240ml)   ○○○○○○○○○○○○○○○○

DATE:		WEEK:		WEIGHT:	

Warm Up/ Stretching Duration:

Exercise		Set 1	Set 2	Set 3	Set 4	Set 5
	Weight					
	Reps					
	Weight					
	Reps					
	Weight					
	Reps					
	Weight					
	Reps					
	Weight					
	Reps					
	Weight					
	Reps					
	Weight					
	Reps					
	Weight					
	Reps					
	Weight					
	Reps					
	Weight					
	Reps					
	Weight					
	Reps					
	Weight					
	Reps					

CARDIO WORKOUT

Exercise	Duration	Pace	Heart Rate	Calories

WATER   1 cup per circle
(1 cup = 8 ounces ~ 240ml)   ○○○○○○○○○○○○○○○○

DATE:		WEEK:		WEIGHT:	

Warm Up/ Stretching	Duration:	

Exercise		Set 1	Set 2	Set 3	Set 4	Set 5
	Weight					
	Reps					
	Weight					
	Reps					
	Weight					
	Reps					
	Weight					
	Reps					
	Weight					
	Reps					
	Weight					
	Reps					
	Weight					
	Reps					
	Weight					
	Reps					
	Weight					
	Reps					
	Weight					
	Reps					
	Weight					
	Reps					
	Weight					
	Reps					
	Weight					
	Reps					

CARDIO WORKOUT

Exercise	Duration	Pace	Heart Rate	Calories

WATER   1 cup per circle
(1 cup = 8 ounces ~ 240ml)   ○ ○ ○ ○ ○ ○ ○ ○ ○ ○ ○ ○ ○ ○ ○ ○

DATE:	WEEK:	WEIGHT:

Warm Up/ Stretching   **Duration:**

Exercise		Set 1	Set 2	Set 3	Set 4	Set 5
	Weight					
	Reps					
	Weight					
	Reps					
	Weight					
	Reps					
	Weight					
	Reps					
	Weight					
	Reps					
	Weight					
	Reps					
	Weight					
	Reps					
	Weight					
	Reps					
	Weight					
	Reps					
	Weight					
	Reps					
	Weight					
	Reps					
	Weight					
	Reps					

CARDIO WORKOUT

Exercise	Duration	Pace	Heart Rate	Calories

WATER   1 cup per circle
(1 cup = 8 ounces ~ 240ml)   ○○○○○○○○○○○○○○○○○

DATE:	WEEK:	WEIGHT:

Warm Up/ Stretching   Duration:

Exercise		Set 1	Set 2	Set 3	Set 4	Set 5
	Weight					
	Reps					
	Weight					
	Reps					
	Weight					
	Reps					
	Weight					
	Reps					
	Weight					
	Reps					
	Weight					
	Reps					
	Weight					
	Reps					
	Weight					
	Reps					
	Weight					
	Reps					
	Weight					
	Reps					
	Weight					
	Reps					
	Weight					
	Reps					

CARDIO WORKOUT

Exercise	Duration	Pace	Heart Rate	Calories

WATER   1 cup per circle
(1 cup = 8 ounces ~ 240ml)   ○ ○ ○ ○ ○ ○ ○ ○ ○ ○ ○ ○ ○ ○ ○ ○

Made in the USA
Middletown, DE
05 February 2020